Crochet for Beginners stiches.

CROCH

FOR BEGINNERS

If You've Decided To Master Crocheting In a Cheap Way, Here's A Simple Visual Step By Step Grandmother's Guide:

Be A Pro Crocheter In Less Than 21 Days!
Part 2 Includes Bonuses

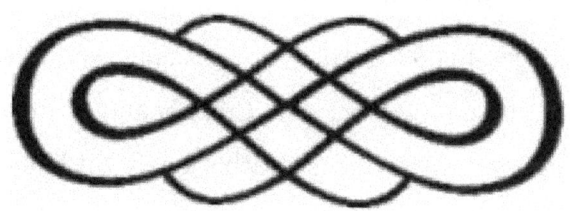

By Kate Stevens

Table of Contents

Introduction to Crochet 6
What Is Crochet? 6
Crochet History 7
Crochet Supplies 16
Useful Things To Know About Your Crochet Equipment 19
Sizes 19
Yarn 19
Crochet Goal 21
Techniques for crochet are also common activities. 21
Crochet Stitch Patterns 22
Crochet Patterns 23
Where to Find Crochet Patterns 23
How to Read a Crochet Pattern 23
Similarities and Differences between Crochet and Knitting 24
Who Can Crochet? Could You? Is Crochet the Right Hobby for You? 24
What is the single crochet foundation (fsc)? 26
Start the Row 28
Make the Chain a part of the stitch. 28
Start the unmarried Crochet a part of the stitch 28
End the Single Crochet Part Of the Sew 29

Get Prepared For the Following Sew 29

Make the next FSC. 29

Keep Crocheting Your Task 31

Afghan crotchet sew. 32

Afghan Hooks 32

Afghan sew mission Examples. 33

Crochet the Tunisian Crochet Base Row. 34

Start Crocheting the Tunisian Crochet Base Row 34

Work In The Front Or The Start Chain Back. 35

Begin the Forward Pass crochet. 35

Number the crochet rows in Tunisian. 36

The Afghan Stitch's full line. 37

Wrap Over The Loop The Thread. 37

Repeat the Stitches. 38

Whole the Go Back Bypass. 38

Quit Your Afghan Sew 38

Tunisian knit sew. 40

Workout This Crochet Stitch 40

Running the Knit Stitches in Tunisian Crochet 43

WHERE TO PLACE THE STITCHES . 45

Extra guidelines for analysing Crochet symbol Charts 49

WHAT YOU NEED TO KNOW TO BE ABLE TO READ CROCHET SIGNS 51

Studying a Crochet sample 52

Understanding the Crochet 55

Working in Rows.. 56

How to Read a Crotchet Chart Sign 57

What Are The Crochet Symbol Charts? 57

HOW TO READ THEM. 60

CROCHETING A PICOT STITCH 61

Small Picot Stitch 61

Crocheting the seeds stich. 64

A way to crochet inside the spherical shape. 67

How to Crochet a Checkerboard Stitch... 71

How to crochet a crazy shell stich 75

How to create a pop-corn stitch.. 80

How to Crochet a Shell Stitch... 85

How to Crochet a Treble Stitch 87

This guide contains several photos that will support you make a treble stitch. Employ this guide and afterwards teach everyone else to do this pattern. 87

Steps: 87

How to crochet the magic circle.. 89

Reverse Single Crochet Stitch-Crab Stitch. 93

Tunisian Crochet Stitch. 96

Bauble ended picot stitch: 101

VARIATIONS AMONG KNOTTING AND CROCHETING........................ 104

Similarities.. 104

Elements 105

Knitting components 105

Crochet components 107

Yarn 109

Structural Differences in Material 109

Tasks 110

WHICH IS EASIER? 111

Knit-Like Crochet 112

A WAY TO CROCHET A HEADSCARF FOR BEGINNERS 114

Completed Headband Length 114

Gauge 115

Crochet scarf instructions 116

The Way to End Off 118

How to crochet a double treble stitch (dtr) 119

Insert Hook 120

Yarn Over, Draw via loops on the hook. 120

Yarn Over, Draw Through 120

Keep Repeating Pattern 120

Continue Through the Last Two Loops 120

Whole Double Treble Crochet Sew 121

Guidelines for operating Double Treble Crochet Stitches 121

Conclusion part 2 122

Introduction to Crochet

What Is Crochet?

Crochet is an embroidery method that utilizes a crochet hook with fiber or similar material. This fiber is most usually wool or crochet thread, but it could also be leather, rope, twine, or other inventive content.

Crochet fans are looking forward to finishing crochet creations that are usually useful, desirable, or helpful items in some way. Common initiatives typically involve Afghans, crocheted blankets, baby booties, sweaters, beanies, and squares of granny, shawls, pouches, tote bags, and many others. A number of different things can be crocheted, including brooches, socks, and curtains.

It is also important to use different components in other products to crochet. Crochet trims as well as edgings, for example, are common projects; you may add them to crocheted products, knitted items, as well as sewn pieces (including ready-made shop-bought items), such as purchasing some shoes, towels, and/or pillow cases, and applying a crocheted finish to each.

Crochet History

The term crochet is taken from the Medieval French word croc or croche, which means cord. Crocheting, that means hook basically.

As it was called in English, French, Belgians, Italians, as well as Spanish-speaking individuals, do call crochet. The skill is recognised in Holland as haken, in Denmark haekling, in Norway hekling, and also in Sweden virkning.

Due to archeological finds, historical documents, and artistic renderings of various kinds, certain types of handwork-knitting, lace, and weaving-can be dated well back into time. But whenever and wherever crochet rose to prominence, nobody's really sure.

The phrase comes from croc, or croche, a word for hook in Middle French, and also the word for hook in Old Norse is krokr.

"The modem practice of true crochet as known today was created during the 16th century," says American crochet pioneer and world traveler Annie Potter. "It became popular as' crochet lace' in France and' thread lace' in England."

As well as, she tells us, in 1916, Walter Edmund Roth met ancestors of Guyana Indians then discovered traces of true crochet.

A further writer / researcher, Denmark's Lis Paludan, who restricted her quest for Europe's crochet roots, placed forth 3 interesting thoughts. One: Crochet developed in Arabia, spread east to Tibet and west to Spain, from where it migrated to other Countries on the Arabian trading routes.

Two: Crochet's earliest records originated from South America, where someone said that a native group used crochet decorations in puberty rituals. Three: Early reports of three-dimensional dolls employed in crochet were documented in China.

Yet, says Paludan, the truth of the matter is that there is "no compelling evidence as to how ancient crochet practice might be or where it originated from. Until 1800, it was difficult to find traces of crochet in Europe. Some sources say that crochet was regarded as' nun's job' or' nun's lace' in Italy as far away as the 1500s, where it was employed by nuns for religious textiles,"s.

Crochet for Beginners

Her research has given rise to examples of lace creating some kind of lace tape, most of which have been maintained, but "all indications are that crochet has not been recognised in Italy quite far back as 16th century"-but under no name.

Studies shows that crochet was actually more specifically derived from Chinese needlework, a very ancient form of embroidery found in Turkey, India, Persia, and North Africa that entered Europe in the 1700s and was referred to as "tambouring," from those in the French "tambour" or drum. A backdrop cloth is placed on a plate in this technique.

Under the cloth is kept the working yarn. A needle with a hook is inserted downwards, and through the fabric, a loop of the working thread is drawn. The hook is then inserted a little further along with the loop still on the hook, and then another loop of that same working thread is taken up and waited to form a chain stitch thru the first loop.

The hooks of the tambour were as thin as needles of sewing, so the work had to be done with really fine thread.

Tambour developed in to what the French termed "crochet in the air" at the end of the 18th century when the fabric of the background was discarded, and the stitch worked alone.

Crochet for Beginners

In the early 1800s, crochet started to appear by Europe and was offered a massive boost by Mlle. Riego de la Branchardiere, who has been best remembered for her ability to make crochet variations that could readily be duplicated by taking old-style needle as well as bobbin lace styles.

She authored many trend books in order to start copying her designs by millions of women. Miss. Riego also helped popularize "lace-like" crochet, also named Irish crochet. Irish crochet was a practical lifesaver for the citizens of Ireland.

This lifted them off of their potato famine, which persisted from 1845 to 1850 and plunged them into abject poverty. In those days, comfortable living standards for the Irish were severe.

A wide range of fabrics have been used across the ages: feathers, grasses, reeds, horse hair and sinew, corn, flax, leather, gold and silver and copper fibers, silk, woolen thread, wool yarns (soft zephyr yam, luster yarn, double cable yarn, carpet yarn), cotton yarns (anchor and estramadura), silk threads (cordonnet and floss), linen strings, hemp threads, mohair, chenille, modern mixtures, meta combinations.

We now have a huge selection of linen, wool, silk as well as organic yarns at our fingertips. With these uncommon materials such as copper cable, plastic strips, sisal, jute, fabric scraps, unspun wool, and sometimes even dog hair, we could also crochet.

And what about the device for crochet? We are now going into a yarn shop or Costco and purchasing metal, plastic, or steel hooks in over 25 size options.

Though, in ancient times, they used everything they could get their hands on-first fingers, after which hooks made from metal, wood, fishbone, animal bone, horn, old spoons, teeth of thrown away combs, brass, mother-of-pearl, morse, tortoiseshell, ivory, copper, steel, vulcanite, ebonite, silver as well as agate.

In Dublin at the period of the great purge (1845 to 1850), that at least one individual used to make fine Irish crochet was indeed a needle or a steep wire threaded into a cork or slice of timber or tree bark, with both the end filed down and twisted into a tiny loop.

Person-and it was the men's role-created his craftsmanship for practical reasons in the early centuries. To catching animals as well as snare fish or birds, hunters, as well as fishermen, produced knotted chains of twisted fabrics, cords, or strips of fabric. Other implementations included braided game bags, fishing nets as well as kitchen utensils that were open-worked.

Crochet for Beginners

To important occasions like those of religious ceremonies, holidays, weddings, or funerals, handwork has been extended to include informal decoration. In crochet-like adornments and ornamental drippings for arms, ankles as well as wrists, most of us see ceremonial outfits.

In Europe of the 16th century, aristocracy and the wealthy were adorned in gold trimmings, gowns, hats, headpieces- and the poor folk would only hope of wearing these items. And, it's thought, crochet was created as the emulation of the lace of the rich man by the poor people.

Continuing into the Victorian era, crochet designs were popular for flowerpot holders, bird cage covers, visiting card frames, lamp mats and shades, wastepaper containers, tablecloths, antimacassars (or "antis," covers to shield chairbacks from hair oil worn by men in the mid-1800s), cigarette packs, purses, men's caps, and waistcoats, even a footwarming rug to be put undead.

People were also busy crocheting Afghans from 1900 to 1930, sleeping rugs, walking rugs, chaise lounge, sleigh rugs, vehicle rugs, cushions, coffee and teapot cozies, and hot water bottle coverings. During this period, potholders rendered their first appearances and then became a standard of the arsenal of that same crocheter.

Crochet for Beginners

Then, of course, there is something going on. Crochet started off as an impressionistic medium of communication in the 1960s and 1970s that can now be seen in three-dimensional paintings, textile pieces, or rugs and tapestries portraying abstract and practical patterns and scenes.

Comparing crochet techniques from the past against those we employ today is fascinating. For illustration, it is recorded in the Dutch journal, Penelope, during the period 1824 to 1833 that both the yarn and the hook had to be kept in the hand while holding and the yarn moved from the right forefinger over the hook.

The thread is kept in the right hand as well as the wool in the left in crochet textbooks from the 1840s, as right-handers do now.

In a German publishing dated 1847, it indicated that you should "keep the very same tightness, either crochet crudely or crochet tightly, otherwise you won't achieve an attractive even texture. Moreover, if you don't work on the round, you need to split off your yarn at just the end of each row, as this provides the crocheted item a finer finish." At the flip of the 20th century, this change occurred.

Researcher Lis Paludan theorizes that perhaps the exhortation to retain the same tension "seems to mean that crochet needles are all of the same width and that the crocheter was required to work in the right tension according to fashion."

Ancient design directions, dating back to the mid-1800s, suggested that the hook was only to be used in the second half of the stitch using a single crochet stich.

Jenny Lambert, a German, wrote in 1847 that putting the sole crochet in the back half of that same stitching was useful to make table runners and so on, but running the hook through those loops could be used to "crochet sole for shoes and other things that must be thicker than normal, but the procedure is not ideal for designs."

Another simply copied the work of someone else until ideas were recorded. Specimens were made, sewn and attached like scrapbooks, stitched on large strips of fabric, or left loose in a bag or case. Writer Annie Potter discovered many of these scrapbooks in use by nuns in Spain in her travels, dating back to the late 1800s.

A further way of collecting stitch patterns was to knit various stitches in large, thin bands together-some created by parents, some begun at school then added to it over the years. (Subsequently, in Europe, around 1916 to around 1926, readers were able to buy tiny pattern variations together with their yarn.) In 1824, the first crochet patterns documented to date were printed.

The first designs of color work crochet were for silver and gold silk thread purses.

In many nations, crochet books have been discovered, mostly translated from one language into another. Mlle was perhaps the most popular crochet specialist. Riego de la Branchardiere, who has written over a 100 novels, has released many on crochet.

The crochet publications from the mid-1800s were slim but also included woodcut drawings, only around 4 inches by 6 inches. According to Paludan, these tiny gems included designs for white buttons-like collars, cuffs, lace, insertions including caps for women and kids, along with models for handbags, slippers, and hats for men.

Cotton thread, coil yarn (Scottish thread on spools), linen, or hemp thread is preferred fabrics for white crochet (insertions, edgings, pads, underwear trimming). Silk, wool as well as chenille yarns were recommended for colorwork and also precious metals threads.

Such early designs would make current crocheters nuts, many of which were not correct. For example, an eight-pointed star could turn out to have only six points. It transforms out that the reader was required to read the sequence and to use the depiction as the most precise guide.

Crochet Supplies

Crochet Hook: The first device you need is a crochet needle. Crochet designs indicate the scale of the hooks you need to use. Your boss will help you determine which hooks to use for your first job.

Scissors: Hold a convenient pair of scissors or tweezers for thread clipping, pump cutting, etc. In a protection situation, make sure to maintain scissors.

Yarn: Yarns can be found in a multitude of weights (strand diameter) as well as fiber material. Employ the yarn indicated in the guidance for the best outcomes.

Make sure to buy all of the yarn you want for a design at the very same time as loads of dye will differ somewhat in coloring, and this will be shown on the completed project.

When in the same design you mix different kinds of yarn, make absolutely sure they are

Gauge: Gage is the amount of stitches per inch (and spaces), as well as the couple of rows for every inch. Gauge is defined in many designs over four inches. Your scale will be the same as the gauge defined in the template so that your project is the right size. That's particularly important for initiatives that need to match.

Crochet for Beginners

Think about making a gauge palette again once you start the design. Utilize the same thread, needle, and template stitch as set out in the directions to test the strength. Create a swatch of around 6 inches long. Work around 6 inches in sequence, then attach. And let all the swatch settle a little, then squish it to fit without no stretching.

Use sticks, map off a 4-inch square segment of stitching in the middle of the swatch. Count the amount of stitches as well as rows in this segment of 4 inches. Ye can start immediately in on your design if they fit the scale.

If you've had very few stitches, you're operating too loose— shifting to a small hook and creating another swatch. If you've got just so many stitches, you're working too closely— shifting to a bigger hook.

Continue to make swatches as well as play with hook measurements until you get the required gauge. Different manner, everyone/crochets should help you create a design that suits. Each yarn skein has the size of the yarn and the label's suggested hook. For your future, you'll want to retain the sticker.

Threads are used to knit as well. Crochet yarn is commonly used as a project edge for dollies, place mats, table tops, or table tops. A thread of 10 dimension is the most widely used.

The greater the amount of loops, the better the thread, so finer than 10 is 20, and finer than 20 is 30. You're going to need to use a thread snare to crochet this sort. With a 10-thread dimensions, a "0" hook tends to work well.

Tapestry Needle: For embroidery seams, a blunt spotted sculpture needle is used. It is safer to have a simple, steel needle. Many needles throughout the tapestry have a ridge around the neck. These aren't perfect for crocheting seams as when the hump traps stitches, which makes it difficult to pull thru the thread.

Measuring Tools: You would need a ruler (6 or 12 inches), a tape, or a metal-measuring gage to measure.

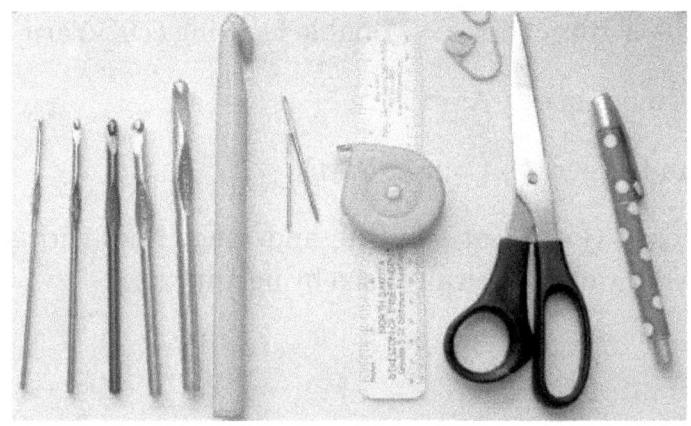

Useful Things To Know About Your Crochet Equipment

Crochet needles come in many shapes and patterns, but how do you select right one?

Sizes

A crochet needle's size is generally determined by a measurement of length, number, or ' mm. ' If they are defined by text, for example, they tend to range between E to J – E becoming the lowest as well as J being the highest.

Yarn

Each crochet needle is designed to operate with a distinct yarn type; the image below shows the weights that work with those of the hooks.

Crochet for Beginners

Hook Size	UK Yarn Weight
2.5mm – 3.5mm hook	4 Ply Yarn
3.5mm – 4.5mm hook	Double Knitting (DK) Yarn
5mm – 6mm hook	Aran Yarn
7mm and larger	Chunky Yarn

A standard G or H needle (the mid-range one) with such a DK weight yarn is typically used by beginners.

Crochet Goal

Crochet fans are looking forward to finishing crochet creations, which are usually useful, desirable, or helpful items in certain way. Popular designs involve Afghans, crocheted blankets, baby booties, scarves, caps, and squares of granny, shawls, belts, tote bags, and many others. A range of different items can be crocheted, from hats, shoes, and curtains.

It is also necessary to use different components in other products. Crochet trims as well as edgings, for instance, are common projects; you may attach these to crocheted products, knitted items, including sewn pieces (including ready-made supermarket-bought items), such as purchasing some shoes, towels, and pillow cases, and applying a crocheted finish to the whole.

Techniques for crochet are also common activities.
Not very many crocheters are obsessed about crochet tasks being done. In addition to the tasks, there are many other objectives, objectives, and incentives of crochet.

The Crochet Base Unit: A Crochet Sew Every crochet design comprises of crochet stitches. The following are the fundamental crochet stitches:

- The chain stitch
- The slip stitch
- The single crochet stitch
- The double crochet stitch
- The half-double crochet stitch
- The treble crochet stitch
- The double-treble crochet stitch
- The triple-treble crochet stitch

Crochet Stitch Patterns

To create unique stitch designs, crochet fans may adapt the simple stitches in unique ways. Multiple different looks can be created; lacy or flat, decorative or translucent, patterned, or simple stitch designs can be used. Many common patterns of crochet stitches are about as follows:

- Shell stitch
- V stitch
- Cluster stitch

Crochet for Beginners

The end result is an unmarried crochet first row that appears even higher than the conventional way of starting.

Here are more than one motives to attempt FSC: the primary row of general unmarried crochet often twists and coils as you spot pictured because it's a good sew. Unmarried crochet base gets rid of this trouble.

You do no longer need to artwork all the one's stitches, only to discover which you miscounted for your beginning chain. With FSC, you could upload or remove or without problems.

In case you need to use the conventional technique, you may nonetheless upload on an additional basis single crochet while wanted.

It feels a hint magical to save a step and assemble your paintings in a modern manner. Who does not like that?

Some styles allow you to realize to apply FSC. However, you could use this even for the ones that don't really make certain to test your gauge and use this approach to your swatch.

Crochet for Beginners

Even as this suggests the proper-handed manner of making your stitches, you may flip those directions if you're left-passed.

Is it equipped to give it a pass? Clutch some yarn and a crochet hook in a size that matches your yarn!

Start the Row
This is all you need to begin your basis chain of unmarried crochet stitches. In case you had been making foundation double crochet stitches, or any other version, you may want to make greater chain stitches in the beginning.

Make the Chain a part of the stitch.
Insert the hook inside the first chain you made.

Make certain to insert it simply, so it catches both the left of the first chain and the centre of the stitch, which ends inside the subsequent chain. You need to see strands of yarn at the left and one on the proper. This is how you may insert the hook on every occasion.

Yarn over and draw up a loop. This counts as making the chain part of the single muse crochet sew.

Start the unmarried Crochet a part of the stitch
You should have two loops on your hook.

Crochet for Beginners

Yarn over and draw up a loop. This is much like the first step in creating single crochet.

You want to have loops for your hook, however.

End the Single Crochet Part Of the Sew

Yarn over and draw the hook thru each loop on your hook. This completes the unmarried crochet.

Get Prepared For the Following Sew

Take a look at your first foundation single crochet.

The stitch you, in reality, drew the loop (at the right issue if you're proper-exceeded) via is the pinnacle of the number one sew and what you will look at whilst counting stitches.

At the opportunity aspect, in an effort to be the bottom, the longer sew is the chain a part of the stitch. This is in which you may insert the hook for the following sew.

Make the next FSC.

Insert the crochet hook into the chain a part of the previous sew.

Crochet for Beginners

Over again, make sure to undergo the chain so that you end up with strands at the left component of the hook. It is a bit much less complicated to look each strand as you upload greater stitches.

Repeat the equal steps from the primary sew. A smooth summary of the stitching machine is going like this:

Insert hook, yarn over, and draw up a loop. Yarn over and draw up a loop. Yarn over and draw via both loops.

Eight paintings vertically for your foundation row.

Despite the fact that most crochet works horizontally from right to left (or left to proper if you crochet left-exceeded), proper here, you can work vertically.

It sincerely is due to the truth the muse single crochet manner is extra like making your beginning chain.

Once you make all the FSC stitches you want to finish the row, you could then turn your artwork and begin as traditional working horizontally.

Keep Crocheting Your Task

Now that you have your first basic row of stitches, you can hold on in your pattern.

What you certainly made counts due to the fact the first row of single crochet, so undergo that in mind in case your sample does not direct you to apply FSC stitches.

As you determine, you can possibly observe that this approach moreover makes it easier to locate in which to work as you move. Its crochet, win-win.

Afghan crotchet sew.

Afghan stitch is easy to crochet sew made using the Tunisian crochet technique.

Afghan stitch goes by means of way of a selection of various names; a few humans additionally name it "Easy Tunisian stitch." you would possibly stumble upon exceptional names for it as properly.

Afghan sew is suitable for crocheting many unique forms of projects, which incorporates garb, home decor, puppy gadgets, toys, and additional.

Afghan Hooks
There are several exclusive styles of crochet hooks you could use for running afghan sew. One of the most popular is an extended, clean hook, measuring at least 10 inches.

Usually, there may be no thumb grip location on an afghan crochet hook. This kind of hook is much like a straight knitting needle as it has the equal type of a stopper at the end.

Crochet for Beginners

You could additionally use a round crochet hook, a double-ended crochet hook, or a hook with a bendy extension on the quit.

Afghan sew mission Examples.
There are various special examples of easy crochet initiatives you could make the usage of the afghan stitch.

Whilst you're finished with this academic, you may be geared up to crochet any of these projects, plus many others.

Top left: Crochet a clean kitchen present set in variegated earth-tone colours. The set consists of potholders and a dishcloth, both of which can be laboured in afghan stitch.

The dishcloth, moreover has an edging of the single crochet stitch.

Top proper: this is a near-up photograph of the crochet stitches.

Decrease left: in case you've in no way worked afghan stitch earlier than, this easy afghan stitch potholder is an outstanding first undertaking to try.

Decrease proper: this is a close-up image of the crochet stitches for the potholder.

Crochet the Tunisian Crochet Base Row.
If you are not already relaxed with retaining your Tunisian crochet hook, you can need to practice.

Start Crocheting the Tunisian Crochet Base Row
If you're already familiar with crocheting, this stitch begins with the same beginning you're used to; you start by making a slip knot, and then you work a chain stitch

Take a cotton yarn skein and a Tunisian crochet hook size J. Chain 30 stitches, then use your finished swatch to create an Afghan stitch potholder like the one pictured when you're finished.

If you're not comfortable holding your crochet hook in Tunisia, you may want to practice it.

Start crocheting the base row of Tunisian Crochet.

If you're already familiar with crocheting, this stitch begins with the same beginning you're used to; you start by making a slip knot, and then you work a chain stitch.

Crochet for Beginners

Take a cotton yarn skein and a Tunisian crochet hook size J. Chain 30 stitches, then use your finished swatch to make an Afghan stitch potholder like the one pictured when you're done.

Work In The Front Or The Start Chain Back.

Working at both sides of the chain, you can see that you have the luxury of operating in the front or in the back. In the beginning, working in the back of the chain can be a bit awkward.

If working in the back of the chain, two loops will be left free so you can finish the project easily; you may want to add an edging, whip stitch through those loops, or use the loops for some other finishing technique.

Begin the Forward Pass crochet.

Use the following sequence to draw a loop into the next chain stitch (the second chain from your thread) and insert your hook into the stitch. Wrap the yarn over the hook and catch it with the hook and pull it through the thread of the chain.

Continue for the Forward Pass to Crochet.

First, in the next chain stitch, you must follow the same exact steps again.

You must repeat this process in your starting chain, pulling up a loop in each stitch of the chain until you reach the end of it.

Number the crochet rows in Tunisian.

You've completed the "forward," also known as the "forward pass" when you've pulled up a loop in each chain stitch. There are some crocheters that say you've completed row 1, while others say you've only completed the first part of row 1. When working, keep in mind that when working on this stitch, it's not a good idea to stop in the middle of a row.

If you want to stop working, both the forward and the return passes are better done before you put down the work. With this method, fixing messed up work is simple, but in some cases, it requires ripping back a little further than you might be used to with non-Tunisian crochet.

Next comes the' return,' better known as the' return pass.' You're going to crochet a chain stitch to continue the return pass.

You're used to crocheting a turning chain between rows if you already know how to crochet. Recall that the thread of this chain is not a turning link. You won't turn over your job; you'll keep crocheting with the same side of the work you're facing.

First, you must start to merge two-stitch groups at a time, as follows: wrap your yarn over your hook and pull it through the next two loops on your thread. Repeat, tie the yarn, and pull it through two more loops around your ring.

The Afghan Stitch's full line.

Continue this process until you've been working all over the row back. You're going to be left with a single loop on your hook at the top.

Now it's time for the next row to continue.

In your next section, you can think of the first stitch as already completed. You wouldn't usually count your active loop as a stitch with non-Tunisian crochet. Here is your next row you have to count it as the first thread.

First, find the vertical bar under your crochet hook. You don't want to work on it. You want to work right next to it in the first vertical slot. If you're right-handed, that would normally be on the left side of it immediately; if you're left-handed, you'd more likely look for it on the right side depending on how you're doing your job.

Wrap Over The Loop The Thread.
You will want to loop your yarn over the crochet hook and pull it through the vertical bar after you put your hook into the vertical bar.

Crochet for Beginners

Continue to repeat this series of steps until the end of the row.

Repeat the Stitches.

If you appear carefully at the surrender of the row, you'll see that there may be a vertical bar there too.

When you achieve the forestall, you may repeat the identical cross lower back pass tested earlier. First, you chain 1; then, you consolidate groups of loops till you high-quality have one loop final in your crochet hook.

A few crocheters talk over with this as "working the loops off with the useful resource of twos," or without a doubt "running the loops off."

Whole the Go Back Bypass.

Entire the move returned bypass. You have to have a pleasant even row even as it's finished.

Quit Your Afghan Sew

This curling is flawlessly ordinary with afghan sew; that is virtually one of the characteristics of this form of material.

You can discover smart strategies of counteracting the curl with this sort of stitch.

In a few cases, turning into a member of portions collectively once more-to-decrease lower back will do the trick. In different instances, including a prominent edging is sufficient to counteract the curl.

The edging doesn't want to be fancy; it could also be a substantial band of undeniable unmarried crochet.

Tunisian knit sew.

Do not let the call fool you. The Tunisian knit sew is not virtually united; it's far definitely crochet sew. It's now best called a knit sew because it looks as if sew (additionally known as a stocking sew) in knitting.

This instructional will train you the way to paintings the Tunisian knit sew, that could be an on-hand sew to recognize in case you'd like your crochet work to resemble knitting.

If you aren't already skilled with Tunisian crochet, you could additionally prefer to discover ways to preserve a Tunisian crochet hook.

Workout This Crochet Stitch
As soon as you have got found out, this sews, be sure to test out more than one amusing responsibilities you can use for working closer to it.

Hint: The Tunisian knit stitch is a notable stitch for the use of all of the ones beautiful, variegated yarns, which is probably available.

Begin With the Tunisian Crochet Base Row.

Crochet for Beginners

There's the first-rate terminology finished to this starting row. Its miles occasionally called the "base row" as well as the "foundation row."

There can be individual names for it as accurately. Rows like this where you're drawing up loops additionally may be called the "forward" or the "in advance skip."

When you have no longer already found out a comfy manner of protective your hooks while you do Tunisian crochet, you may desire to try this first.

To get started, crochet a beginning chain of any duration more than two stitches.

To begin the Tunisian knit sew, you could see paintings into either the front aspect of the decrease lower backside of your beginning chain. It's exceptional to work into the lower back of the beginning chain.

That manner, there is probably loops unfastened to artwork into across the lower part in case you want to function an edging or elaborations for your paintings later. If you test the lower edge of the work in view H, you may see what is supposed by using "loops lose.

Crochet for Beginners

Tunisian Knit stitch pass back, reverse, and pass back skip

The subsequent component has several unique possible names. A few humans name it the "go back" or the "cross lower back pass." some humans call it the "reverse" as nicely.

Even as following different designers' patterns built the usage of this stitch, you could find out that some humans name this "row 2" of the work, even as others envision it as being the second 1/2 of row 1.

To finish the return or different pass for the Tunisian knit sew, artwork a sequence sew with the aid of looping the yarn over your hook and pulling it via the last loop in your catch.

Repeat from all the manner across the row until most straightforward one loop stays on your hook. The closing loop at the hook will rely as the first sew in the subsequent row.

Once more, the terminology for this factor of the technique is not standardized. A few people call this "jogging off the loops," or you can look at instructions telling you to "work off the loops by means of twos."

Others talk over with this as "binding off" or "eliminating," this is possibly how a knitter may particular it; there are precise similarities right here to the manner of binding off in knitting.

Running the Knit Stitches in Tunisian Crochet

If you had been going to work the Tunisian smooth stitch, the following step would be to work stitches into the vertical bars all of the way throughout the subsequent row.

You are now not going to do this here, but the vertical bars create an important frame of reference.

There may be a vertical bar underneath your active loop. However, you can't sincerely do anything with that one, so just neglect approximately it and use the subsequent closest vertical bar as your reference factor.

The usage of your crochet hook, you'll pierce the cloth completely thru from the front to lower back, as established in view R, and the spot to do it is straight away to the proper of the vertical bar.

After you have driven your hook through the fabric, yarn over and pull up a loop. In case your hook went in at the suitable spot, the end result will look something like view S.

Continue pulling up loops on this manner all of the manner for the duration of the row. Running more Rows of Tunisian Knit sew.

Crochet for Beginners

Subsequent, you could repeat the steps for finishing the return pass/opposite; it's miles precisely the equal proper right here as it end up the first time you possibly did it.

To feature extra rows of the Tunisian knit stitch, virtually preserve repeating the steps you already found out.

After you parent the reverse, the paintings will look something like view. Then preserve with drawing up every other row of loops and working them off via twos. Now you're geared up to do the Tunisian knit sew like a professional

WHERE TO PLACE THE STITCHES

The other important thing you really need to remember is where to place the stitches from a crochet symbol map.

You're going to work as usual row-by-row or round-by-round, reading photos rather than words. In general, row-based charts are worked from top to bottom, moving in the same direction that you always crochet.

From the inside out, round-based symbol charts are employed from the middle and counter-clockwise (for right-hand crocheters).

Some charts of symbols have row numbers on each row's right side. The symbol chart often has an arrow (usually a solid black arrow) to show you where to start when a circular pattern is being worked.

Unless the picture tells you otherwise, the stitches in a row go side by side (each put into the next stitch).

For instance, the shell stitch symbol may have five vertical lines coming from one stitch; from the row below, you will position all five stitches in the same stitch.

There are usually arrows or other directions attached to the chart to show this when the stitches are to be applied in any direction that is different from the ordinary.

Symbol chart and key included with free crochet pattern over the Rainbow Crochet Snuggle Sack Typically stitches are worked through both loops.

There are exceptions, however, where only in the front loop or back loop stitches are worked. There is a symbol for each of these variations: a half-circle with the open end facing downwards for the back loop or upwards for the front loop (u-shape).

It helps to remember that the stitch for the front loop lies inside u, nearest to you, and further away from you on top of the hump of an inverted u for the back loop.

You will sometimes fit around posts rather than into stitches, of course. As mentioned above, there is a hook at the bottom of the post stitch symbol that indicates this. The hook is wrapping around the post.

Crochet for Beginners

Lastly, crochet diagrams typically do not indicate whether you are working in a stitch or between stitches in a chain area.

Although their wide range of example of it but where you'd work in the chain spaces, it's only through additional written instructions or your art experience that you'd know how to work in the chain space rather than in the stitch.

For this purpose, if they are usable, it is important to look at the written instructions.

Tip: "Write" Aloud Charts for Practice When you start working with symbol charts at first, it can help you write each stitch aloud when you work to focus your attention on what you're doing.

Take, for example, Linda Permian's crochet symbol chart for the Small Leaf pattern in the Flowering Necklace free crochet pattern: Looking at this picture of the leaf, you see a series of chain stitches and from your crochet experience, you know this is where you continue.

So, you count the symbols of the chain and find there are nine, and you can say "chain nine" to yourself.

When you reach the end of the nine chains, it's time to start your first row. The first stitch you see is a mark of "x," referring to a single crochet stitch.

There's just one of them. Whenever you look closer at it, you see that this is done away from the hook (where you made the final chain of the nine chain stitches) into the third line.

So, you might say to yourself aloud "single crochet in the hook's third row." First, you see that there are two symbols for half double crochet stitches, so you might say, "The half double crochet in each of the next two links."

Each of the next three chains has a double crochet symbol. Say aloud, "In each of the next three strings, double crochet."

Now take a closer look at what is going on in the chart. In the first chain you made (which is on the left of the work), there are eight double crochet symbols.

All of these are put into that one stitch, and it takes you around to the other side to finish row 1 by working on the opposite side of the foundation chain. For now, tell aloud, "the last series of eight double crochets."

Crochet for Beginners

Switch the job so that by working on the opposite side of the foundation chain, you will continue to follow the map. You can see that the work you've already done is a mirror image.

So, you may say aloud, "dual crochet in each of the next three lines, half dual crochet for each of the next two chains, and crochet single in the next section.

Also, this symbol chart should have a slip stitch symbol, though it doesn't. You'd slip stitch to the first single crochet to close the leaf and then fasten off your job.

Extra guidelines for analysing Crochet symbol Charts

Remember to check the pattern key for the image chart before starting the work.

 Although maximum designers use the standard symbols adopted by way of the Craft Yarn Council, a few patterns may use extraordinary stitches, so it's constantly first-rate to double-check.

 Be aware that maximum symbols correspond to US crochet terms, but some patterns, specifically the ones written by way of UK crochet designers, may correspond to UK crochet terms.

Crochet for Beginners

Dabbles and Babbles has a clear chart displaying how the symbols correspond to the US vs. united kingdom terms.

Practice operating from charts which have accompanying written instructions.

Folks that already understand how to examine commands can use this as a method of double-checking their paintings as they analyse.

Paintings from the image chart, however, refer back to the written instructions to verify which you're working correctly.

Note the colour of the chart. Commonly, a crochet pattern laboured in rows could have symbols in one shade on right facet rows (frequently black) and in some other colour (blue or crimson, typically) for incorrect facet rows.

Crochet for Beginners

WHAT YOU NEED TO KNOW TO BE ABLE TO READ CROCHET SIGNS

As an alternative, you could find that a sample has handiest numbered the right-side rows (the ones which can be worked right to the left in a right-passed sample) or that the proper-facet rows are calibrated very well on the right and the wrong side rows at the left.

• Mark off your rows as you pass. Speaking of keeping the music of where you're in a sample, it could be helpful to mark off the rows as you go so you do not lose song of your vicinity in the paintings.

This could be accomplished with marks at the diagram or by using a row counter.

You could additionally want to apply to sew markers within the physical paintings to track your stitches and rows.

In case you do get lost, appearance carefully at your material and the diagram; they must appear the same as one another, so once in a while, you could locate your area visually.

Notice: although the words are often used interchangeably, there is commonly a difference between crochet charts, crochet graphs, and crochet diagrams.

Charts commonly consult with the image charts mentioned in this text. Graphs commonly check with the block-like visual instructions utilized in niches like filet crochet and tapestry crochet.

Diagrams often seek advice from meeting/layout commands.

Reading crochet patterns can be totally daunting for novices, what with all those letters and numbers looking like hieroglyphics.

But in case you understand how to interrupt your sample down, it is tons simpler to decipher.

Those are the pointers to get you started out — hold them handy, and shortly you will be able to examine any pattern like a seasoned.

Studying a Crochet sample

As soon as you've got selected your sample, sit down, and appearance it over to make sure you absolutely apprehend what the venture needs. Most crochet styles have the subsequent sections:

Crochet for Beginners

- An "approximately" section that has sample notes
- Yarn, substances, and notions wished
- Data on gauge, anxiety and/or sizing
- Abbreviations used
- Any special stitches used

These all provide useful (and often important) info you need to know before you start. Allows dig into them a touch extra.

Be aware of which crochet terms are used on this segment, as there are international differences between phrases used in the U.S. and the U.K. You need your pattern to be written within the terminology you're used to.

Yarn, materials, and Notions
Make sure you check vividly to ensure that you have all the yarn and different substances you want.

In case you're the usage of more than one skeins of yarn that have one-of-a-kind dye lot numbers, you have to recognise how to control them to avoid awkward and accidental colour versions.

Gauge

Except you're making a scarf or blanket, usually, always, always make a gauge swatch earlier than you start your venture.

Now you need to test your gauge. First, use a ruler to test how many stitches throughout in shape into 4" (you must have 14).

Then, test what a number of rows healthy into 4" (this has to be 7). In case your numbers are correct, you have got the precise gauge.

In case your gauge is off, there are approaches you could restoration it.

So, you may say aloud, "dual crochet in each of the next three lines, half dual crochet each year for the next two chains, and crochet single in the next section.

Understanding the Crochet

Crochet diagrams are a game-changer. They show you exactly what stitch you're the use of and wherein it goes at a look.

Definitely positioned, a diagram is a chart or schematic of a pattern made of symbols that constitute stitches. As soon as which stitch the symbol represents, there's no stopping you.

Even better: diagrams are created using across the world recognized symbols that corresponded to each sew and guidance. In other phrases, they allow you to crochet in any language.

Commonly, diagrams are used for edging, borders, and for repeating sew patterns. They're also on hand for illustrating what distinct stitch mixtures look like.

For some of the simplest stitches, the graph above displays the symbols. The diagram from which you work should provide a reference, but don't sweat it if it doesn't, the symbols are universal.

What this key tells us is that a stitch is defined by each symbol. And if you really dig deep, it makes sense for the symbols: the dc symbol has one horizontal bar to reveal a yarn over, and the try has two bars for two yarn over.

Often, the symbols are about to scale: single crochet is smaller than a double crochet hook. It means that your diagram is a pretty accurate representation of what it will look like when you're finished.

Working in Rows

First things first: Diagrams are labored from the bottom up and are designed for right-exceeded crocheters unless in any other case, noted.

Allows observe the stitch diagram for Granny stitches Rows above.

• Begin at the lowest left, working your basis chain.

Then, you may paintings row 1, reading the sample from right to left. Then, turn your paintings, and sew across row 2, studying from left to right.

• The stitches stack on top of each different so that you can see what sew to artwork into as you cross up the sample.

• A bracket that has been shown on the right side of the diagram shows the variety of rows within the sample repeat.

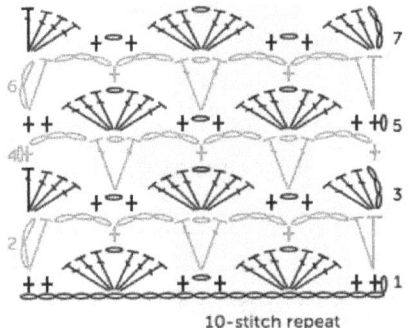

10-stitch repeat

How to Read a Crotchet Chart Sign

Crochet instructions can be written in text (with or without abbreviations) and/or graphed or charted in symbols. Reading symbol charts expands your options to work with different crochet pattern types. This guide describes how to interpret the charts of crochet.

What Are The Crochet Symbol Charts?

A Symbol Chart is a visual representation of a crochet pattern. Each row or round is represented using symbols representing the stitches, stitch by stitch. The Council of Craft Yarn has introduced a set of uniform crochet symbols that are widely used across all crochet designs.

The symbols in the chart are designed to look like simple stitch representations; once you've been used to seeing them, they'll be as plain to you as the written crochet abbreviations you see in patterns.

You know "sc" means single crochet, and you'll find out that a symbol of x or + also means single crochet.

The image above for the five double crochet shell is shown right here within the higher right nook of the stitch.

This image additionally consists of the visible design of the stitches as well as the written commands

Symbol charts, provide a visible opportunity to written commands for crochet symbols. There are numerous motives why this may be useful:

1. Many crafters are visible freshmen. There are numerous one of a kind ways to learn, and a number of human beings find picture-based instructions simpler to recognize than text-based guidelines.

Make the craft easier on yourself if you're a visual learner with the aid of getting to know a way to examine charts.

2. Charts beautify written commands. In many cases, a crochet sample consists of each written and symbol commands.

Crochet for Beginners

You could normally discover it smooth to examine text guidelines; however, in some cases, it is able to be helpful to have a look at the visible to make feel of specific portions of the sample.

It's far greater information that may be beneficial.
Three image charts aren't language-based. Once the way to read crochet image charts, you may be capable of observing them on every occasion they're to be had.

This lets in you to get crochet books in different languages (eastern crochet books are popular, for example). You shouldn't know the way to examine the written language in case you share the common language of crochet.

A be-aware for Left-handed Crocheters

As we continue into the info of analysing image charts, it is critical to be aware that maximum charts are written for right-exceeded crocheters.

That the pattern must be reversed for left-surpassed crafters. This can be completed mentally or thru physical reproductions.

HOW TO READ THEM.

When you get acquainted with the symbols that represent every stitch, it is fairly easy to study image charts.

They're designed to read precisely as they look, so the fabric that you are creating on your arms will look similar to the visible diagram on the web page.

There are key things to learn while studying image charts: what the sew is and where it is going.

- There are traces to symbolize "yarn overs." The double crochet sews like the 1/2 double T with a single "hatch" line across the bar.

This line represents that it has one "yarn over" to make the double crochet. The treble crochet seems similar but with two hatch lines representing the 2 "yarn overs" that start this stitch.

- Brackets are used to suggest sew pattern repeats. Many designers additionally encompass the phrase "repeat" to signify the location to repeat and the wide variety of times to achieve this.

- Colours are commonly indicated with the aid of the letter. The Ogee stitch Afghan loose Crochet sample includes a list of materials that indicates which letter corresponds with which shade.

CROCHETING A PICOT STITCH

Typically, the Picot Seam is used as an outline, applied to a completed fabric. Take this guide and start making 3 stitches of picot.

Small Picot Stitch:

1. Operate across a completed item's bottom. (To add a picot side length to something like a ready-to-wear item, start with a sole crochet or dual crochet strip.)

2. Single crochet inside the first stitch.

3. Chain three, single crochet in the subsequent stitch.

4. Single crochet inside the subsequent three stitches. Chain three, unmarried crochet inside the subsequent stitch. (Picot fashioned).

Crochet for Beginners

5. Repeat step 4 throughout the row.

Low stitch of Picot:

1. Follow the tiny picot stitch instructions, but chain five as opposed to chain 3.

3. Do the sequence of unmarried crochet, chain five, single crochet in the same stitch to make a slightly flared picot side as shown in the image to the right one.

3. This could barely pop out and will support the bottoms of tank tops, or skirts, on sleeve edges, or caps.

Crocheting the seeds stich.

This seven-step tutorial shows you how to crochet the stitch of seed. The seed stitch is a single and double crochet stitch that alternates. It offers a closed stitch that looks like a stitch of knitted thread.

- Begin with a chain. Turn, single crochet from the hook in the second stitch.

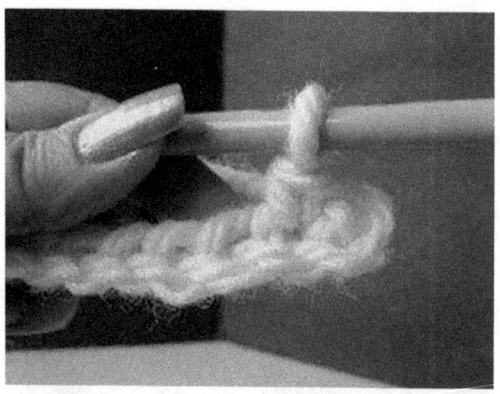

- Dual crochet in the next stitch.

- Single crochet in the next stitch.

- Iterate steps two as well as three across the row.

- One line of seed stitch accomplished.

- Turn at the end of the line when you ended up in double crochet, the first stitch of single crochet.

Slip stitch in the first line, chain 2, (takes the place of the first double crochet), simple crochet in the next stitch, when you finished in single crochet.

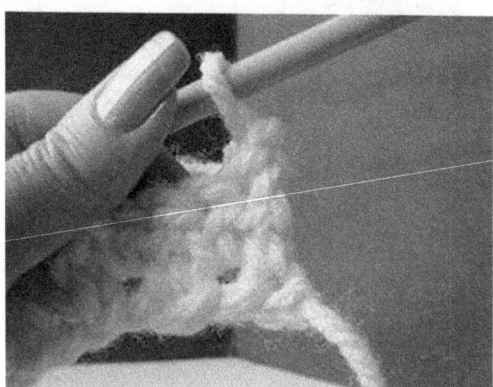

- Go through the row, alternating with a single crochet in the previous row's double crochet, and vice versa. Photo shows 3 rows of completed seed stitch.

Crochet for Beginners

A way to crochet inside the spherical shape.

This is a splendid little by little educational that teaches you a way to crochet within the spherical shape.

Steps:

1. Chain a hoop on which to build your crochet inside the round: chain 5, slip stitch to join.

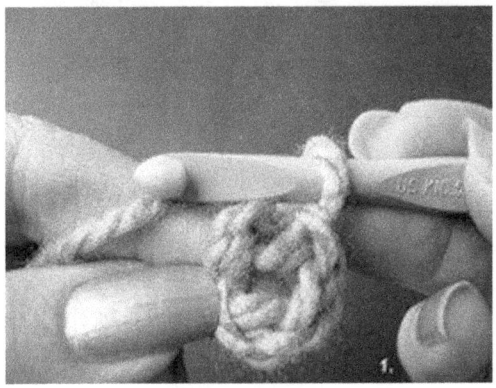

1. Chain 2 to begin to double crochet.

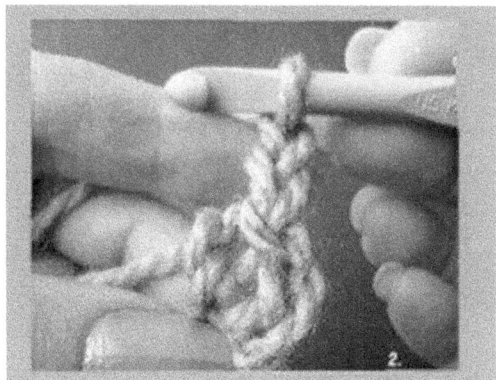

- Consider the number of double crochet stitches needed for the round. 10 Double crochet in this case, plus chain 2...

- Fifth and sixth. Slip to touch the thread. At the beginning of the string, slip stitch into the top of chain 2.

Crochet for Beginners

- Chain 2 to begin following round of stitches.

- Switch the job in the opposite way. (You can also spiral crochet in the round, so you don't turn.)

- Finish the crochet stitches needed for that round. (You're going to increase the stitches in each round in about any case.)

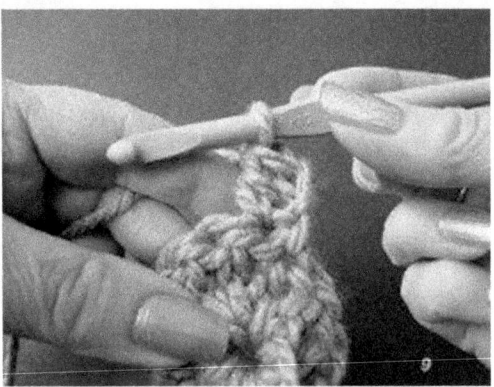

- Slip stitch to join the round.

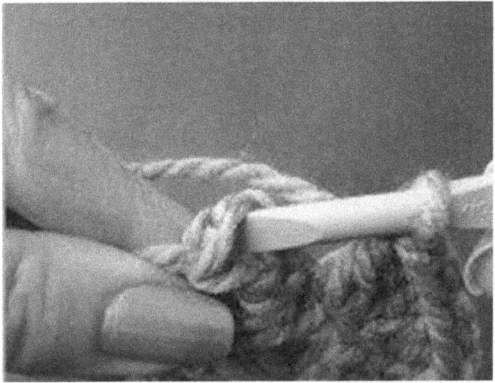

- In attempt to provide an invisible edge, shut that stitch to slip the stitch in.

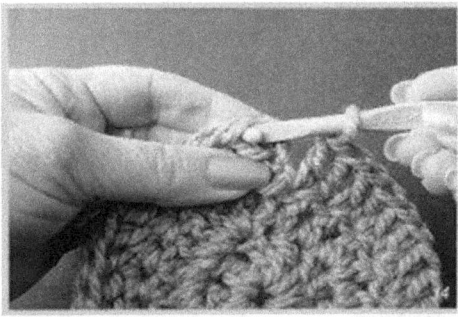

The arrow points to the right stitch to reach the slip stitch. Slip stitching in the wrong stitch is the most common error in the round's crochet. Image 15's arrow points to the right stitch to reach the slip stitch.

How to Crochet a Checkerboard Stitch

The stitch of the checkerboard is a really good stitch. For a very neat-looking afghan, you can use just one for a dishcloth or knit the squares together. It's a perfect step by step guide to this tutorial.

- Begin with a chain. Dual crochet at the hook's third stitch and at the next stitch

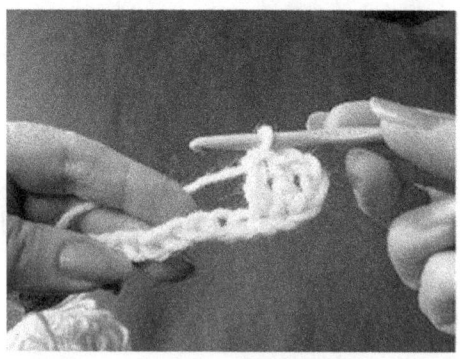

- Chain 3.

- Jump the following three stitches. Make Double crochet in each of the next three seams.

1. Repeat steps 2 and 3 across the row. Always end with a double crochet in the last stitch.

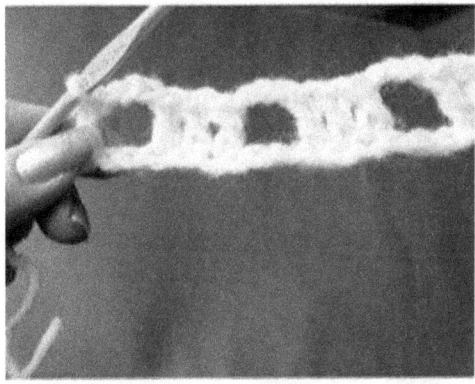

- Chain 3 and turn.

- Create 2 dual crochet in the preceding row's chain 3 room. (Chain 3 is the very first dual crochet instead.)

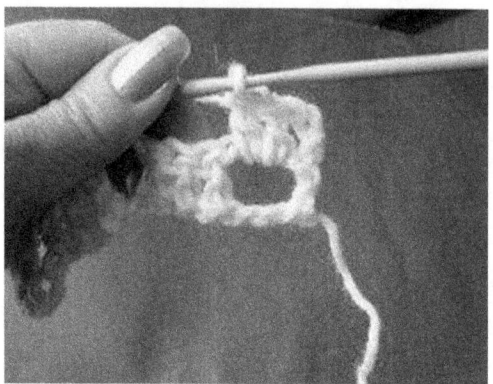

- Chain three, make three dual crochets in the space of chain 3 of the preceeding row.

2. Repeat step 6 across the row.

3. Photo shows 3 rows of checkerboard stitch completed.

How to crochet a crazy shell stich

Follow this step-by-step guide to learn how to make a mad stitch of mesh. You start with multiples of three in a chain first, but in the tutorial, you can read that. This is a lovely stitch you're going to want to know.

1. Start with a line, plus one extra in multiples of three. 15 + 1, or 18 + 1, or 21 + 1, for instance. Make 3 double crochet from the hook at the 4th stitch.

- Leave the three subsequent stitches, sole crochet in the next stitch.

Crochet for Beginners

Chain 3

Make 3 double crochet in the same stitch, skip the next 3 stitches, single crochet in the next stitch.

Repeat from * across the row. End with a single crochet.

- Second Line: Chain three and make the turn. Make three dual crochets in the sole crochet of the preceeding row. (The same stitch as the chain three just made.)

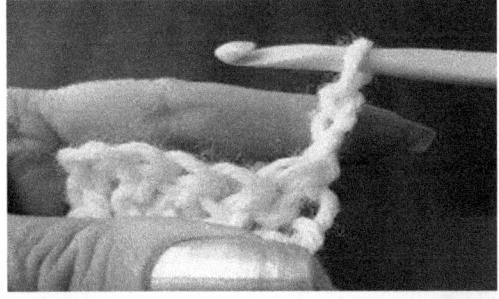

Simple crochet in Three place over the next row. (You'll notice it on the opposing side of that same previous row's next dual crochet cluster.)

Chain three, make three dual crochet in the same chain three space. Single crochet in the next chain 3 space.

Repeat from across the row three Repeat the second Row until your achieve the required size of your project.

How to create a pop-corn stitch

It is quite simple when you have the correct instructions on how to do that. All you do is render in the same row a series of dual crochet stitches. This brilliant guide is going to be showing you how.

- Set a set of pillars that can be separated by Three solo crochet from the needle and in every loop of the set in the second thread.

- Chain One then switch, solo crochet over the next Two stitches. Create Five dual crochet stitches over the next row, holding each stitch's last chain on the thread.

Crochet for Beginners

- Insert the stitch into all of the six loops on the hook.

- Solo crochet in three subsequent stitches.

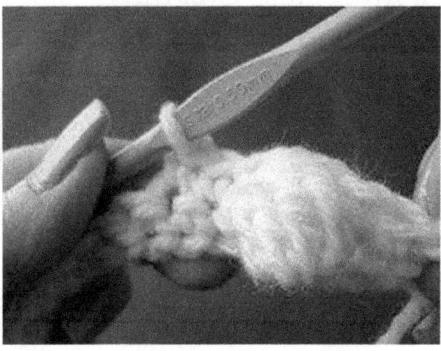

- Iterate steps two, three, then four across the row, beginning the step two.
- Chain 1 and turn, single crochet in each stitch across the row. (In the popcorn stitch, single crochet in the center stitch.)

(Single crochet in the centre stitch of the rear of the popcorn stitch.)

7. Iterate the following steps two, three, four then five for the number of rows required to complete your project

(2 rows of popcorn stitch completed)   (3 rows of popcorn stitch completed.)

How to Crochet a Shell Stitch

To know how to make crochet of a shell stitch, obey this seven-step tutorial. This stitch can then be used in any method you want.

- Begin with a chain.

- Dual crochet it in the third seam taking from hook.

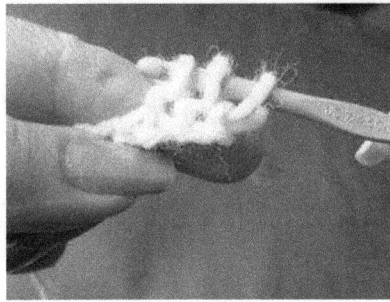

- Make 4 more double crochet stitches in the same stitch.

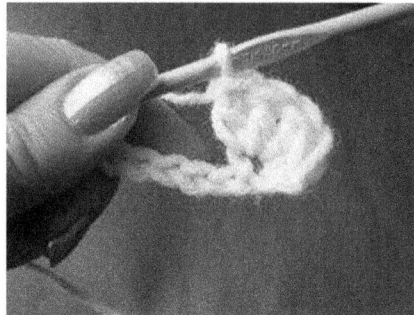

- Skip the next 3 stitches, make 5 double crochet in the next stitch.

- Repeat step 4 across the row.

- At the end of the row, turn, slip stitch in the first 3 stitches, chain 2, make 4 double crochet in the same stitch. Then repeat step 4 across the row.

- Iterate step six for each following row of the shell stitch.

How to Crochet a Treble Stitch

This guide contains several photos that will support you make a treble stitch. Employ this guide and afterwards teach everyone else to do this pattern.

Steps:

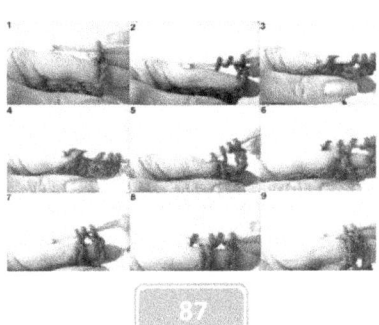

Crochet for Beginners

1. To start to make a row of treble crochet, first chain 3.

2. Yarn over the hook 2 times. (3 loops on the hook.)

3. Insert the hook into the next stitch.

4. Hook onto the yarn.

5. Pull through the stitch. (4 loops on the hook.)

6. Hook onto the yarn.

7. Pull through 2 loops. (3 loops remaining on the hook.)

8. Hook onto the yarn.

9. Pull through 2 loops. (2 loops remaining on the hook.

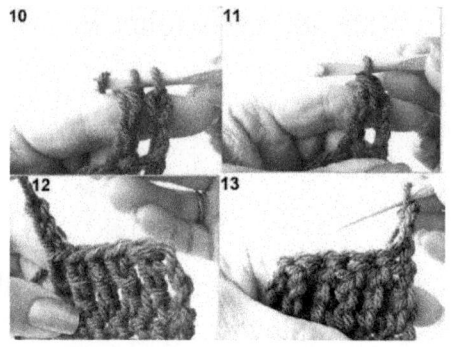

10. Hook onto the yarn.

11. Pull through the last 2 loops on the hook (1 loop remaining on the hook.) Repeat steps from 2 to 11 for each treble crochet.

12. At the end of the row of treble crochet, chain 3.

13. Turn the work to begin working on the next row.

NOTE: Always insert the hook into the second stitch of the row, as the chain 3 is equivalent to the first treble crochet of the row.

How to crochet the magic circle

There are several ways to get around going. The magic circle is one of those ways. You will pull the hole closed by the magic circle. To learn this stitch, follow this tutorial.

There are several ways to get started when crocheting in the round. You can join chain 4, slip stitch, and make a loop.

You can chain three and make double crochet stitches from the hook in the 3rd stitch, or you can continue with the magic circle. In the middle of your work, the first two approaches would leave a hole.

The' Magic Circle' lets you open the closed door.

First, begin in the same way as usual in crochet to make the magic circle.

Create a loop.

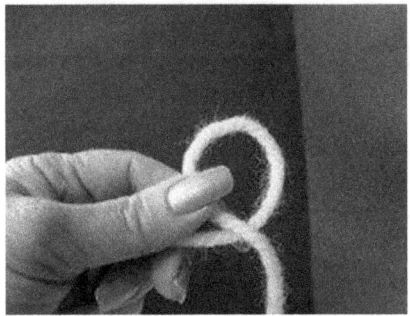

Pick up the yarn.

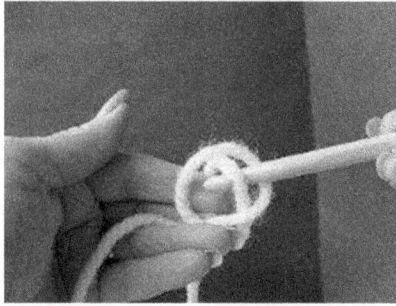

Pull through the first loop.

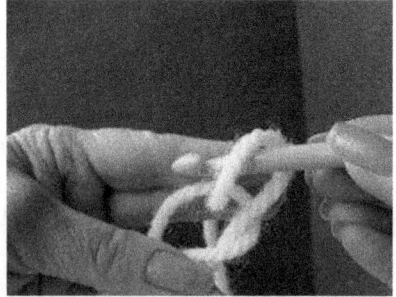

Pick up the yarn again, to make a chain stitch.

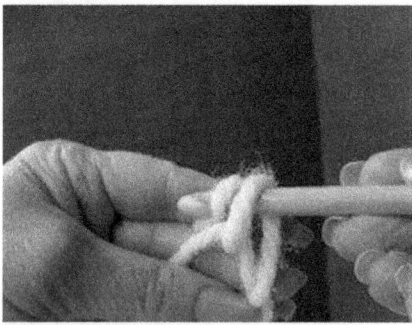

Pull through the loop. (Chain stitch completed.)

Crochet for Beginners

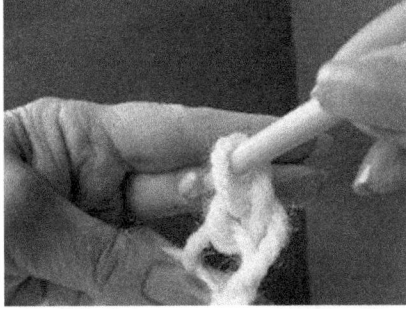

Pick up the yarn again to begin a single crochet stitch.

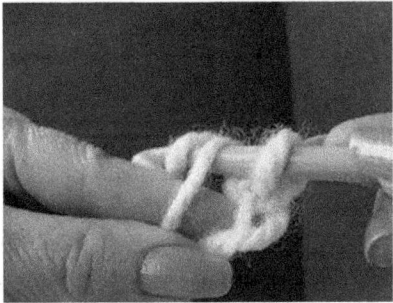

Pull through the loop.

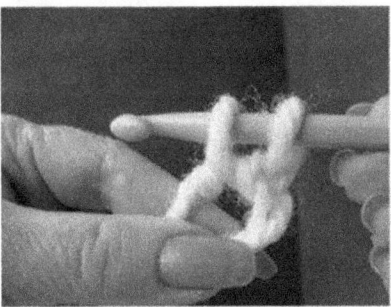

Pick up the yarn again, and finish the single crochet stitch.

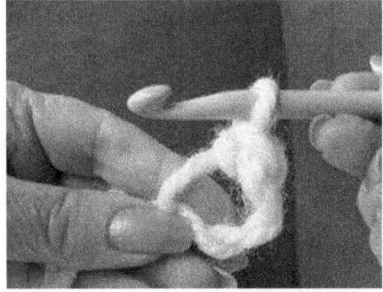

Continue to make single crochet stitches in the main loop.

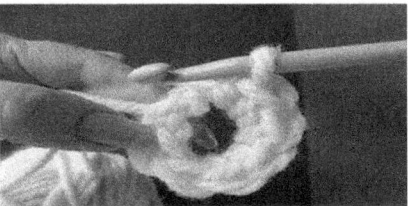

At the end of the round of single crochet stitches, pull on the yarn end to gather the hole closed, and continue with your pattern.

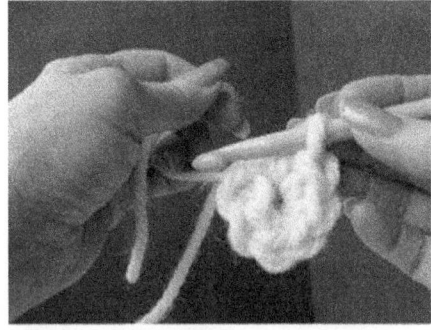

Photo below shows the magic circle finished, with the hole gathered closed.

Crochet for Beginners

Reverse Single Crochet Stitch-Crab Stitch.

The reverse single crochet stitch for finished projects is a flexible stitch to create a Bouillon bottom.

For the edges of Afghans, place-mats, or other square things that need a more significant edge, you may learn this stitch. This is a tutorial that is easy.

1. After completing a row of single crochet stitches, do not turn.

2. Do not turn the work. Insert the hook back into the 2nd last stitch completed.

Crochet for Beginners

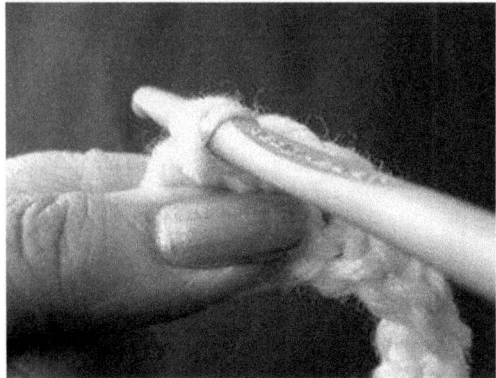

3. Yarn over, and pull through the stitch, just as you would for a single crochet.

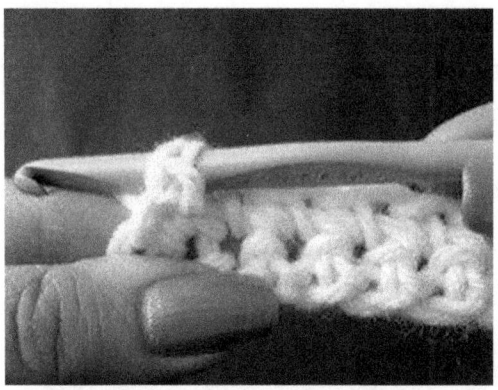

4. Yarn over again, and pull through the two loops on the hook.

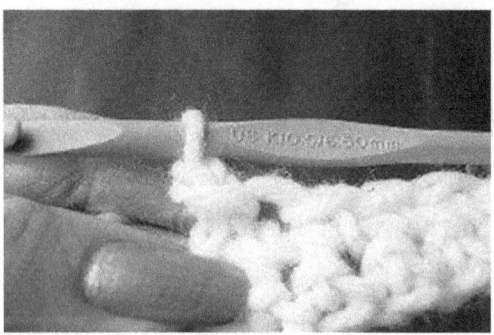

5. Insert the hook into the next stitch.

6. Yarn over, and pull through.

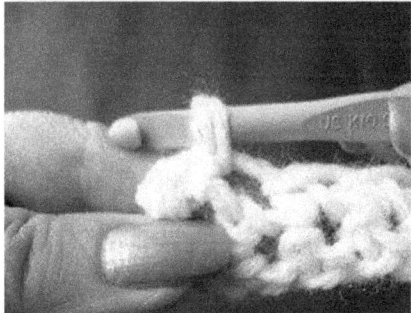

1. Yarn over, and pull through the two loops on the hook.

8. Continue making the reverse single crochet across the row, and the end result is a lovely, coiled style edge to your finished projects.

Tunisian Crochet Stitch.

Many names are known for the Tunisian crochet stitch: Afghan stitch, Railroad knitting, hook, knitting, crochet knitting, shepherd's knitting. To learn the popular Tunisian crochet stitch, follow this step-by-step tutorial.

If you don't have a traditional Tunisian crochet hook, which is a very long-handled crochet hook, then Tunisian crochet is really only practical to make smaller items like wallets, headbands, belts, and other small items that don't require more than a dozen stitches across the line.

That's because all the stitches are staying on the hook, and they're going to fall off the hook's back end!

So, the first chain as many stitches as your project needs to start Tunisian crochet.

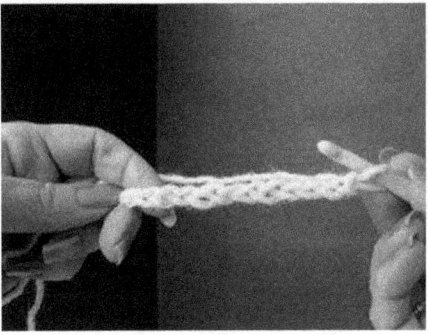

Then work back down the chain as if you were making the first half of a single crochet, but keep the loop on the hook as you go down the line. You'll have as many loops on your hook at the end of the line as your chain.

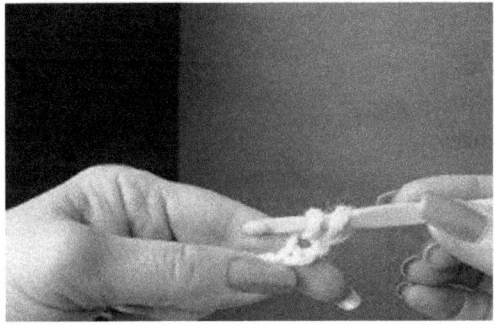

Crochet for Beginners

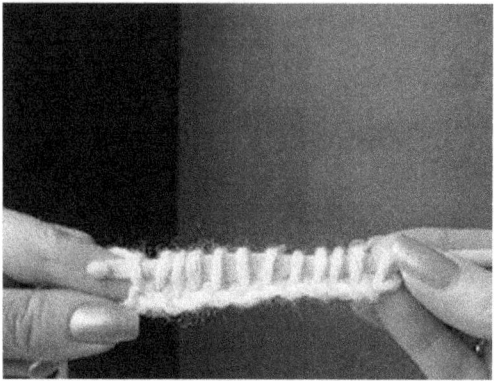

And if you've got a 13-stitch chain, you're going to have 12 line loops.

Now, don't turn the job, yarn over, just pull 2 loops through. Repeat from across the entire row until there is just one loop left on the hook.

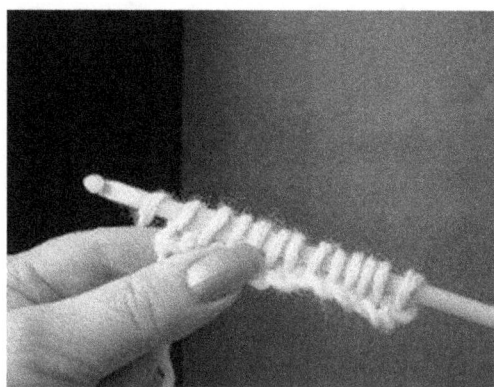

Crochet for Beginners

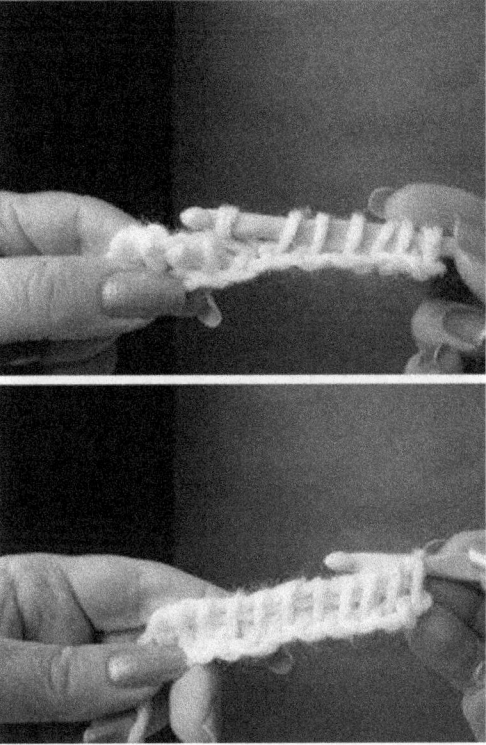

Now, at every point, you're going back down the line, picking up a loop. (Pass the hook through the stitch and go directly to the other side (second picture below).

Count the number of hook loops in each row to establish the proper number of stitches

Crochet for Beginners

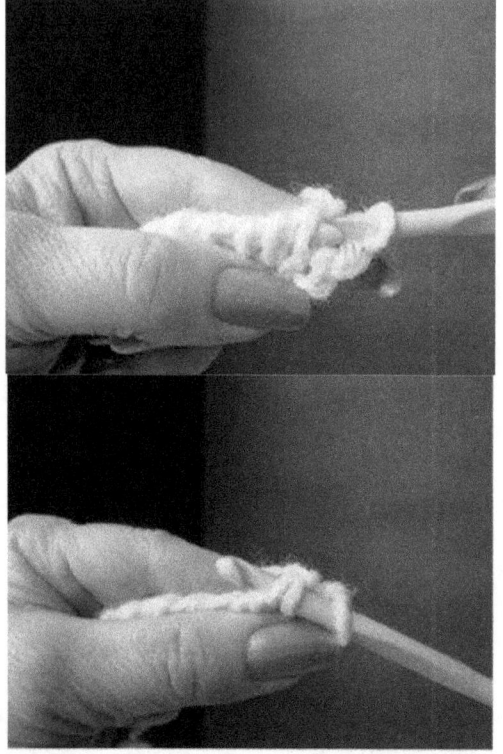

Yarn over, pull forward, keep the loop on the line.

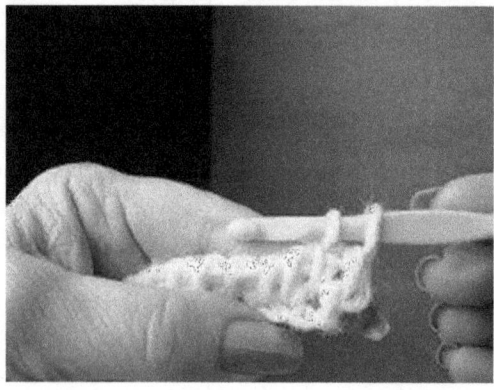

Continue down the row.

Crochet for Beginners

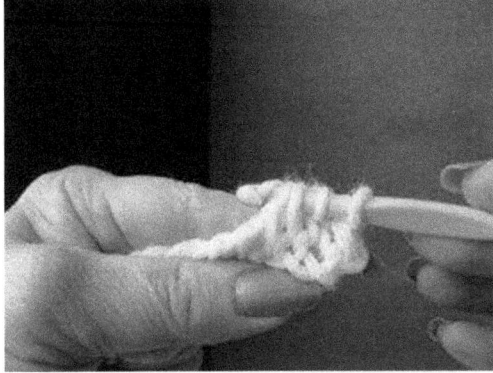

- Four rows of tunisia completed sequentially

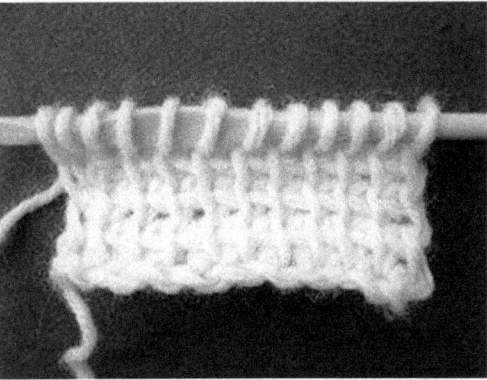

- this is a tunisia snitch been view from the back

Bauble ended picot stitch:
- Follow the commands for the small picot sew, except chain 7 as opposed to chain three.

- Slip stitch from either the hook at the 6th stitch.

- Slip stitch at the chain's last loop. Over the next 3 stitches, solo crochet.

Crochet for Beginners

4. Repeat steps one, two and three across the row.

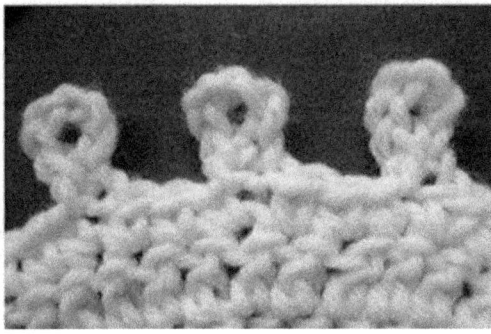

VARIATIONS AMONG KNOTTING AND CROCHETING.

People who are strange with yarn crafting frequently confuse knitting and crochet. It is absolutely understandable that this happens; those crafts share many similarities and not unusual elements. However, they also have big sized differences.

Similarities

Each craft utilizes yarn or fibre, and you could make the equal kinds of projects inclusive of sweaters, shawls, wraps, blankets, Afghans, scarves, hats, mittens, socks, and so on. With either method.

Knitting and crocheting each require similar skill sets: hand-eye coordination, an eye for colour and layout, an affinity for fibre.

The capability to devise an undertaking from start to finish and see it via the mathematical potential is helpful, even though not strictly important, for both craft technique.

Each knitting and crochet offer a number of extremely good health benefits.

Principally, each knitter and crocheters need to have the endurance necessary to maintain running, stitch after stitch after stitch, until a task is finished.

So what is the difference between knitting and crocheting? Why wouldn't it be counted whether or not you do one, or the alternative?

It would not always remember, beyond private choice, of the route, but the ones folks who might just get to know and have a little interested in yarn crafting will want to discover the variations between the two crafts for better information of which one is probably perfect to them.

Right here are some of the each's differences:

Elements
With regards to substances, knitters and crocheters come to be with comparable yet special stashes; you may discover most of the differences inside the equipment department.

Knitting components
A few knitters—hand knitters, this is—use pointy knitting needles. The sharp needles can appear in several unique types of configurations; they often exist in units of, although this is not constantly the case.

From time to time, the two needles are related by using a wire, as in the case of a circular knitting needle.

Now and again they come in units of extra than two. As an instance, double-pointed sock knitting needles regularly come in sets of four or five.

If pointy needles are a part of the manner, then the crafter in query is knitting with the aid of hand.

Hand knitters are simplest a subset of the full quantity of knitters. In addition, handy knitters, there are also looming, knitters and device knitters.

There are numerous unique types of looms and machines that can be used for knitting; they range from the easy to the complex, from the small to the huge.

A few small machines may be used to knit in-wire socks or diverse other small initiatives.

There are larger machines that may be used to knit sweaters, clothes or different similar projects.

Then there are large circular machines, some of which would not even suit in the living room of a median domestic, that mass-produce knitted fabric for the fabric company

Knitting machines promote very well the production of knitted fabrics from very exceptional threads and yarns. As an instance, t-shirt material is normally knitted.

Due to the fact crochet must be achieved by using hand, and it's tedious to apply such first-rate threads for crochet paintings, it is rare to locate crocheted cloth as lightweight and "drapery" as knitted t-blouse cloth.

(That said, there are a few first-rate strategies in crochet that do make it feasible to make crochet t-shirts. It's no longer not possible; it's just something that can be.

Crochet components
Crocheters are not using pointy needles or machines to make their tasks; they use a single crochet hook.

The hook may be small or huge, or any size in among. It'd usually be made from steel, aluminium, and bamboo, plastic, wooden or bone, but it is honestly a nice hook.

Crochet is usually completed with the aid of hand, by no means by means of the gadget. A crocheter's moves are so intricate that, to this point, no one has been able to create a gadget that may reproduction them.

There may be something in the fashion industry. This is referred to as a crochet system, but it does not sincerely make the same stitches like the ones made in crochet.

They devise blanket stitches that mimic crochet; however, upon closer examination, it is simple to peer that it isn't always without doubt crochet.

So, to recap, crochet has executed the usage of an unmarried crochet hook and is usually finished by hand in place of with a gadget.

This, the use of a crochet hook as opposed to needles or a system is what makes the sizeable distinction among the two crafts. But the difference in gear consequences in other variations as nicely.

Yarn

There are numerous distinct styles of yarn, and they can all be used similarly in knitting as in crochet, even though a few fidgety yarns lend themselves better to one craft or the other.

Thread is normally reserved for tiny crochet needles; it is no longer something stated an awful lot in knitting.

There is a long-standing rumour that crochet makes use of up appreciably greater yarn than knitting; however many human beings have tested this, and it remains debatable as to whether or no longer it's far proper.

Structural Differences in Material

There are crucial structural variations between crocheted fabric and knitted material.

Each crochet and knitting has yarn loops that are controlled.

With (weft) knitting (the kind of knitting that's closest to crochet if this kind of part can be said to be), the loops build on each other in a way that requires a few lively loops to stay on the needles.

Every sews rely on the help of the sew beneath it; if a knitter drops a sew, the complete column of stitches underneath it might unravel.

With conventional crochet, there usually are not many lively loops at one time—commonly only one loop, or in all likelihood a few loops.

(There are exceptions to this in a few superior stitches and niches of the crochet along with broomstick lace).

The stitches construct on top of every other, but the energetic loop is the most effective spot from which the fabric is prone to unravelling. So, knitting tends to get to the bottom of extra than crochet; frogging is simpler in crochet than in knitting.

Tasks

Its miles impossible to objectively speak which technique is "higher" for any given form of undertaking.

The fact is, the "pleasant" approach for any given assignment comes right down to private choice. Each of those needlework techniques is well worth mastering, understanding and the usage of.

One motive that this query is so not unusual is that the variations in strategies were lots more mentioned lower back while yarns have been so extraordinary and limited.

The approach of knitting with needles allowed for more drape and a higher match, so humans usually used knitting for clothes and crochet for such things as blankets or desk runners.

That's no longer the case, these days, although, due to the fact the variety of both materials and advanced crochet techniques makes it possible to create all of the identical objects that can be made with knitting.

An awesome example is with socks. Socks was once something best knitters made, but now there are plenty of crochet sock styles.

WHICH IS EASIER?
Ask this question of ten distinct yarn crafters and get ten special responses.

Many humans agree that crochet is an easier craft to examine as it calls for simplest the usage of the dominant hand. But, considering the second one hand is used to help feed the yarn in crochet, it is not this easy.

Many humans do certainly locate that crochet is easier to choose up. But simply as many humans who have tried both crafts discover that it's less difficult to knit.

Humans have a tendency to select one over the opposite after working towards each, but there are also people who revel in each equally. People who strive one and locate it tough may additionally need to attempt the alternative to see if it suits them better.

Knit-Like Crochet

Individuals who aren't acquainted with knitting or crochet typically cannot inform the difference among the two at a look.

Folks that craft in one or both of these forms easily come to understand the stitches which are from knitting and people that may most effective be completed in crochet.

However, the variations among the 2 are more and tougher to discover thanks to a number of strategies that permit crocheters to create knit-like fabric.

Tunisian crochet is the maximum famous of those. Its miles a form of crochet that uses multiple hooks hung on longer hooks (and occasionally even round double-ended hooks!) to create knit-like cloth.

Other approaches to creating knit-like fabric with crochet are via knocking or thru running inside the 0.33 loop in half of the double crochet. After which there are a few crafters who combine knitting and crochet in one item; which includes crocheting an edging on a knit garment.

The opportunities are limitless whether or not you need to include crochet or knitting or each!

A WAY TO CROCHET A HEADSCARF FOR BEGINNERS

Crochet patterns don't get any less complicated than this one! That is pretty much the maximum primary crochet headscarf sample you could ask for, which makes it the proper crochet accent pattern for novices.

Not most effective is that this pattern a smooth way to make a headband; however, it is also written for those who don't have a great experience studying crochet styles.

There are not abbreviations, and there are loads of pointers that will help you alongside the way.

Completed Headband Length
This headscarf measures 84 inches (seven toes) lengthy by way of 4 inches extensive. Scarves can vary in size without changing function, so do not worry if yours isn't quite identical. You may analyze as you pass.

Gauge
Eight crochet stitches = three inches.

While it's tempting to jump proper in and begin making the headscarf, it is desirable to get into the real and genuine habit of checking your gauge.

To try this, crochet a gauge swatch measuring as a minimum four inches square (larger is better).

Make the swatch in single crochet sew the usage of the precise same yarn and crochet hook you'll use to crochet your headscarf.

When you have more than eight stitches in line with three inches, it approaches that your stitches are smaller than deliberate and your headband might be smaller than the example. Try making a brand new swatch with a bigger crochet hook.

Likewise, if you find which you have fewer than eight stitches in step with three inches, it approaches your stitches are large than deliberate.

Crochet for Beginners

If so, your scarf is in all likelihood to show out lots longer than intended; you furthermore may chance jogging out of yarn on account that large stitches will burn up extra yarn and create a bigger headband.

Strive to make a new swatch with a smaller crochet hook.

Crochet scarf instructions

Pull out a length of yarn measuring at the least six inches or longer; go away this duration unworked and make a slip knot after that point.

Then, running with the give up attached to the ball of yarn, crochet an extended beginning chain of 224 chain stitches

Row One: paintings a single crochet stitch within the 2d chain from your hook.

After crocheting your chain, you may have a lively loop nevertheless in your hook. Do not count your lively loop. Begin counting with the first chain after the lively loop.

Keep operating single crochet stitches all the way throughout your beginning chain. Work one unmarried crochet sew into each chain stitch till you reach the stop.

Crochet for Beginners

Whilst you get to the cease, count the single crochet stitches to make sure you have a total of 223. Again, sew markers are beneficial here.

Next, crochet one chain sew at the top of the row to apply as a turning chain. Then, flip your paintings horizontally so you can see paintings back across the piece.

Row: when you have a look at the top of the row of unmarried crochet stitches you made, you will see that every stitch has loops at the pinnacle. When you paintings your single crochet stitches from this point on, be cautious to paintings through both of those loops collectively.

Working thru each loop, work crochet sew into the remaining unmarried crochet sew you made in row one. Keep running one single crochet sew into every single crochet stitch, all the way across the row.

Make certain to be counted your stitches and make certain you've got 223 stitches in the row.

(Bear in mind to apply to sew markers to help maintain your remember accurate—preserving depend is so important for a hit task!) Paintings one chain stitch on the end of the row and turn the work over so that you can find paintings lower back across once more.

Rows 3 and Up: Repeat Row till your scarf is the desired width. While you crochet the remaining row, do not paintings a turning chain afterwards due to the fact now it is time to complete your paintings rather than turning it over and continuing.

The Way to End Off

Leave duration of yarn at the quit measuring at the least six inches. Reduce the yarn, taking care now not to drop your active loop.

Wrap the cut period of yarn around your hook, grab it with the hook, and pull it all the way via the energetic loop.

Supply it a gentle tug to make sure that it is tight and will not come undone. Thread the reduce give up of this yarn onto a tapestry needle and use it to weave to your ends.

After you weave in each end, you may wear your scarf or deliver it as a gift!

How to crochet a double treble stitch (dtr)

Basic crochet stitches include unmarried crochet, double crochet, and treble crochet.

They are among the first stitches novices research, and they're observed in maximum crochet styles.

The use double treble crochet stitch (also known as double triple and abbreviated as DTR) is some other simple sew it really is the subsequent step up in peak from the treble crochet stitch.

Tall stitches have specific features, but they may be created in an identical way as the other primary stitches. So if you recognise a way to crochet double or treble crochet sew, the double treble stitch certainly requires a few more steps.

Yarn over three times
Whilst you're equipped to crochet a double treble crochet sew, step one is to yarn over the hook three times.

This makes sense while you keep in mind the other simple crochet stitches. As an example, while you make a double crochet stitch, you yarn over once.

While you make a treble crochet stitch, you yarn over two times. Because the double treble is the following tallest stitch, it is only herbal that you will yarn over three times.

Insert Hook
Insert the hook into the next stitch where the double treble crochet stitch is to be created.

That's exactly what you'd do to make a double crochet stitch or treble crochet, and you're just making the stitch bigger from step one with that extra "yarn over."

Yarn Over, Draw via loops on the hook.
Loop the yarn over the hook and draw via two of the loops in your hook—leaving four loops on the hook. Essentially you are repeating step 3 with fewer loops left at the hook every time.

Yarn Over, Draw Through

Keep Repeating Pattern

Continue Through the Last Two Loops

Whole Double Treble Crochet Sew
Repeat steps one to seven to create an entire row.

You will see that you may see notable stitch element with a stitch of this top

Guidelines for operating Double Treble Crochet Stitches
At the end of a row of treble crochet, you may chain five to turn.

You could use the double treble when crocheting in the remaining loop (the loop made whilst a sew executed in the again loop most effective) of a stitch numerous rows under.

The double treble is likewise often used whilst crocheting a front or lower back publish stitch around the point of another sew numerous rows under.

The double treble crochet stitch may be very flexible, and gaining knowledge of this approach will come up with getting admission to greater difficult styles.

In case you're developing a design, you could use this sew whilst a protracted chain is wanted.

You can also use it to make an undertaking a good way to crochet quick, or while you need larger breaks in the weave.

Conclusion part 2

This book: **CROCHET FOR BEGINNERS** *Learn step by step Crocheting with picture illustrations, Crochet patterns and stitches (Quick and easy guide) Part 2;*

It isn't just a manual about crochet stiches for beginners, it's also contains advisory parts on how to go about crocheting and tools etc.

Take the details herein and sail in your interest for crochet stiches.

CPSIA information can be obtained
at www.ICGtesting.com
Printed in the USA
BVHW091247161120
593417BV00009B/1164